The
SiX NATiONS
Rugby Songbook

The SiX NATiONS Rugby Songbook

y Lolfa

First impression: 2010
Third impression: 2012
© Y Lolfa Cyf., 2010

Every effort has been made to trace and contact copyright holders where applicable in order to gain permission for the use of lyrics. Please contact Y Lolfa if you believe the book includes material of yours that has not been acknowledged, and every effort will be made to correct this in future reprintings.

Illustrations: Siôn Jones

ISBN: 978-1-84771-206-6

Printed on acid-free and partly recycled paper and published and bound in Wales by Y Lolfa Cyf., Talybont, Ceredigion SY24 5HE
e-mail ylolfa@ylolfa.com
website www.ylolfa.com
tel 01970 832 304
fax 832 782

Fields of Athenry

By a lonely prison wall,
I heard a young girl calling:
'Michael, they are taking you away,
For you stole Trevelyn's corn,
So the young might see the morn.
Now a prison ship lies waiting in the bay.'

Chorus:
Low lie the fields of Athenry,
Where once we watched the small free birds fly.
Our love was on the wing.
We had dreams and songs to sing.
It's so lonely 'round the fields of Athenry.

By a lonely prison wall,
I heard a young man calling:
'Nothing matters, Mary, when you're free.
Against the famine and the Crown
I rebelled, they cut me down.
Now you must raise our child with dignity.'

By a lonely harbour wall,
She watched the last star falling,
As that prison ship sailed out against the sky.
Sure she'll wait and hope and pray
For her love in Botany Bay,
It's so lonely 'round the fields of Athenry.

(Pete St John)

The Wild Rover

I've been a wild rover for many a year,
And I've spent all my money on whiskey and beer,
But now I'm returning with gold in great store,
And never will play the wild rover no more.

Chorus:
And it's no, nay, never,
No, nay, never, no more
Will I play the wild rover,
No never, no more.

I went to an alehouse I used to frequent,
And I told the landlady my money was spent.
I asked her for credit, she answered me, 'Nay,
Such custom like yours I can get any day.'

I took from my pocket ten sovereigns bright,
And the landlady's eyes opened wide with delight,
She said, 'I have whiskeys and wines of the best,
And the words that you told me were only in jest.'

I'll go home to my parents, confess what I've done,
And I'll ask them to pardon their prodigal son.
And when they've caressed me as oft times before
I never will play the wild rover no more!

Danny Boy

Oh Danny boy, the pipes, the pipes are calling
From glen to glen, and down the mountain side;
The summer's gone, and all the roses falling
'Tis you, 'tis you must go and I must bide.
But come ye back when summer's in the meadow
Or when the valley's hushed and white with snow,
'Tis I'll be here in sunshine or in shadow,
Oh Danny boy, oh Danny boy, I love you so.

But when ye come, and all the flowers are dying
If I am dead, as dead I well may be,
You'll come and find the place where I am lying
And kneel and say an 'Ave' there for me.
And I shall hear, tho' soft you tread above me
And all my grave will warmer, sweeter be,
For ye shall bend and tell me that you love me
And I shall sleep in peace until you come to me.

(Frederick Weatherly 1848-1929)

The Flower of Scotland

O flower of Scotland,
When will we see your like again,
That fought and died for
Your wee bit hill and glen
And stood against him,
Proud Edward's army
And sent him homeward
Tae think again.

The hills are bare now
And autumn leaves lie thick and still
O'er land that is lost now
Which those so dearly held
And stood against him,
Proud Edward's army
And sent him homeward
Tae think again.

Those days are passed now
And in the past they must remain
But we can still rise now
And be the nation again
That stood against him,
Proud Edward's army
And sent him homeward
Tae think again.

(Roy Williamson 1936-1990)

Loch Lomond

O wither away my bonnie May
Sae late and sae dark in the gloamin?
The mist gathers gray o'er moorland and brae.
O wither sae far are ye roamin?

Chorus:
O, ye'll tak the high road and I'll tak the low.
I'll be in Scotland afore ye.
For me and my true love will never meet again
By the bonnie, bonnie banks o' Loch Lomond.

I trusted my ain love last night in the broom,
My Donald wha' loves me sae dearly.
For the morrow he will march for Edinburgh toon,
Tae fecht for his king and Prince Charlie.

O, well may I weep for yestreen in my sleep.
We lay bride and bridegroom together.
But his touch and his breath were as cold as the death,
And his heart's blood ran red in the heather.

As dauntless in battle, as tender in love,
He'd yield ne'er a foot tae the foeman.
But never again frae the fields o' the slain
Tae his Moira will he come by Loch Lomond.

The thistle may bloom, the king hae his ain,
And fond lovers will meet in the gloamin,
And me and my true love will yet meet again
Far above the bonnie banks o' Loch Lomond.

Scotland the Brave

Hark! When the night is falling.
Hark! Hear the pipes are calling,
Loudly and proudly calling, down through the glen.
There where the hills are sleeping,
Now feel the blood a-leaping,
High as the spirits of the old Highland men.

Chorus:
Towering in gallant fame,
Scotland my mountain hame,
High may your proud standards gloriously wave,
Land of my high endeavour,
Land of the shining river,
Land of my heart for ever, Scotland the brave.

High in the misty Highlands,
Out by the purple islands,
Brave are the hearts that beat beneath Scottish skies.
Wild are the winds to meet you,
Staunch are the friends that greet you,
Kind as the love that shines from fair maidens' eyes.

Far off in sunlit places,
Sad are the Scottish faces,
Yearning to feel the kiss of sweet Scottish rain.
Where tropic skies are beaming,
Love sets the heart a-dreaming,
Longing and dreaming for the homeland again.

(Cliff Hanley 1922-99)

La Marseillaise

(Note: only the first and sixth verses are usually sung at official ceremonies.)

Allons enfants de la Patrie,
Le jour de gloire est arrivé !
Contre nous de la tyrannie,
L'étendard sanglant est levé !
L'étendard sanglant est levé !
Entendez-vous dans les campagnes
Mugir ces féroces soldats ?
Ils viennent jusque dans nos bras
Égorger nos fils et nos compagnes !

Chorus:
Aux armes, citoyens !
Formez vos bataillons !
Marchons ! Marchons !
Qu'un sang impur
Abreuve nos sillons !

Amour sacré de la Patrie,
Conduis, soutiens nos bras vengeurs !
Liberté, Liberté chérie,
Combats avec tes défenseurs !
Combats avec tes défenseurs !
Sous nos drapeaux que la victoire
Accoure à tes mâles accents !
Que tes ennemis expirants
Voient ton triomphe et notre gloire !

(Claude Joseph Rouget de Lisle 1760-1836)

Literal translation:
Come, children of the Fatherland,
The glorious day has come!
The bloody flag of tyranny,
Is raised against us.
Is raised against us.
Do you hear, in the countryside,
The roar of these savage soldiers?
They come right into our arms
To cut the throats of your sons and your wives.

Chorus:
To arms, citizens!
Form your battalions.
Let us march! Let us march!
That our fields may run red;
Steeped in tainted blood.

Sacred love of the Fatherland
Guide and support our vengeful arms.
Liberty, beloved liberty,
Fight with your defenders;
Fight with your defenders.
Under our flags, may victory
Rush to your manly strains;
So that as your enemies are dying
They might see your triumph and our glory!

Non, Je Ne Regrette Rien
(I Regret Nothing)

Non, rien de rien,
Non, je ne regrette rien,
Ni le bien qu'on m'a fait,
Ni le mal, tout ça m'est bien égal.

Non, rien de rien,
Non, je ne regrette rien,
C'est payé,
Balayé, oublié,
Je me fous du passé.

Avec mes souvenirs,
J'ai allumé le feu,
Mes chagrins, mes plaisirs,
Je n'ai plus besoin d'eux,
Balayées les amours,
Avec leurs trémolos,
Balayées pour toujours,
Je repars à zéro.

Non, rien de rien,
Non, je ne regrette rien,
Ni le bien qu'on m'a fait,
Ni le mal, tout ça m'est bien égal.

Non, rien de rien,
Non, je ne regrette rien,
Car ma vie car mes joies,
Aujourd'hui, ça commence avec toi.

(Michel Vaucaire 1904-1980)

Literal translation:
No, nothing at all,
No, I regret nothing,
Neither the good things
Nor the bad, they are the same to me.

No, nothing at all,
No, I regret nothing,
It's been paid for,
Swept away, forgotten,
I don't give a damn about the past.

My memories,
I have burnt my memories,
My sorrows, my pleasures,
I don't need them any more.
Swept away the love affairs
And all their tremblings,
Swept away forever,
I start anew.

No, nothing at all,
No, I regret nothing at all,
Neither the good
Nor the bad, they are all the same to me.

No, nothing at all,
No, I regret nothing at all,
For my life, for my joys,
Today, they start with you.

Inno di Mameli
(Hymn of Mameli)

Fratelli d'Italia,
L'Italia s'è desta,
Dell'elmo di Scipio
S'è cinta la testa.
Dov'è la Vittoria?
Le porga la chioma,
Chè schiava di Roma
Iddio la creò.

(repeat)

Stringiamci a coorte,
Siam pronti alla morte.
Siam pronti alla morte,
l'Italia chiamò.

(repeat)

Sì!

(Goffredo Mameli 1827-1849)

Literal translation:
Brothers of Italy,
Italy has awoken,
With Scipio's helmet
Binding her head.
Where is Victory?
Let her bow down,
For God has made her
Rome's slave.

(repeat)

Let us join in a cohort,
We are ready to die.
We are ready to die,
Italy has called.

(repeat)

Yes!

God Defend New Zealand
(Aotearoa)

(1st verse: Maori
2nd verse: English)

E Ihowā Atua,
O ngā iwi mātourā,
Āta whakarongona;
Me aroha noa.
Kia hua ko te pai;
Kia tau tō atawhai;
Manaakitia mai
Aotearoa.

God of Nations at Thy feet,
In the bonds of love we meet,
Hear our voices, we entreat,
God defend our free land.
Guard Pacific's triple star
From the shafts of strife and war,
Make her praises heard afar,
God defend New Zealand.

(Thomas Bracken)

The 'Ka Mate' Haka

The haka begins with the leader shouting the following five preparatory instructions before the whole team joins in:

Ringa pakia!	Slap the hands against the thighs!
Uma tiraha!	Puff out the chest.
Turi whatia!	Bend the knees!
Hope whai ake!	Let the hip follow!
Waewae takahia kia kino!	
	Stamp the feet as hard as you can!

Ka Mate! Ka Mate!	It is death, It is death
Ka Ora! Ka Ora!	It is life, It is life
Ka Mate! Ka Mate!	It is death, It is death
Ka Ora! Ka Ora!	It is life, It is life

Tēnei te ta ngata pūhuru huru	
	Behold! There stands the hairy man
Nāna nai i tiki mai whakawhiti te rā	
	Who will cause the sun to shine!
Upane... Upane!	One step upwards, another step upwards!
Upane Kaupane!	One step upwards, another step upwards!
Whiti te rā!	The sun shines!
Hī!	Rise!

Advance Australia Fair

Australians all let us rejoice,
For we are young and free;
We've golden soil and wealth for toil,
Our home is girt by sea;
Our land abounds in Nature's gifts
Of beauty rich and rare;
In history's page, let every stage
Advance Australia fair!
In joyful strains then let us sing,
'Advance Australia fair!'

(Peter Dodds McCormick)

Waltzing Matilda

Once a jolly swagman camped by a billabong
Under the shade of a coolibah tree,
And he sang as he watched and waited 'til his billy boiled,
'You'll come a-Waltzing Matilda with me.'

Waltzing Matilda, Waltzing Matilda
'You'll come a-Waltzing Matilda with me.'
And he sang as he watched and waited 'til his billy boiled,
'You'll come a-Waltzing Matilda with me.'

Down came a jumbuck to drink at that billabong,
Up jumped the swagman and grabbed him with glee,
And he sang as he shoved that jumbuck in his tucker bag,
'You'll come a-Waltzing Matilda with me.'

Waltzing Matilda, Waltzing Matilda
'You'll come a-Waltzing Matilda with me.'
And he sang as he shoved that jumbuck in his tucker bag,
'You'll come a-Waltzing Matilda with me.'

Up rode the squatter, mounted on his thoroughbred,
Down came the troopers, one, two, three,
'Where's that jolly jumbuck you've got in your tucker bag?'
'You'll come a-Waltzing Matilda with me.'

Waltzing Matilda, Waltzing Matilda
'You'll come a-Waltzing Matilda with me.'
'Where's that jolly jumbuck you've got in your tucker bag?'
'You'll come a-Waltzing Matilda with me.'

Up jumped the swagman and sprang into the billabong,
'You'll never catch me alive,' said he,
And his ghost may be heard as you pass by that billabong,
'You'll come a-Waltzing Matilda with me.'

Waltzing Matilda, Waltzing Matilda
'You'll come a-Waltzing Matilda with me.'
And his ghost may be heard as you pass by that billabong,
'You'll come a-Waltzing Matilda with me.
Oh, you'll come a-Waltzing Matilda with me.'

(Andrew Barton 'Banjo' Paterson)

God Bless Africa

(1st verse: Xhosa and Zulu
2nd verse: Sesotho
3rd verse: Afrikaans
4th verse: English)

Nkosi sikelel' iAfrika
Maluphakanyisw' uphondo lwayo,
Yizwa imithandazo yethu,
Nkosi sikelela, thina lusapho lwayo.

Morena boloka setjhaba sa heso,
O fedise dintwa le matshwenyeho,
O se boloke, O se boloke setjhaba sa heso,
Setjhaba sa South Afrika - South Afrika.

Uit die blou van onse hemel,
Uit die diepte van ons see,
Oor ons ewige gebergtes,
Waar die kranse antwoord gee.

Sounds the call to come together,
And united we shall stand,
Let us live and strive for freedom,
In South Africa our land.

English translation:
God bless Africa,
Lift her horn on high,
Hear our prayers.
God bless us
Who are your people.

God save our nation,
End wars and strife.
Protect us, protect our nation
Our nation, South Africa – South Africa.

Ringing out from our blue heavens,
From our deep seas breaking round;
Over everlasting mountains
Where the echoing crags resound.

Foreword

I always look forward to February. After the joys and frivolities of Christmas and New Year, it's still cold and dark, everyone's broke and spring seems a long way off yet. We all need cheering up with a good game of rugby, a few beers and the chance to sing some rousing songs to shake off those winter blues. Thankfully, the Six Nations comes around at the perfect time.

The Six Nations is more than just a rugby tournament. It's about history and tradition, loyalty to one's country and the chance to get one over the old enemy. There are scores to settle and pride to maintain. It's a chance for players to prove their worth in a cauldron of tension and emotion.

But what would the tournament be without the passion of the national anthems and traditional songs which get the blood pumping before kick-off? Whoever you support, and whether you're watching the game in the pub, at home, or in the stadium itself, *The Six Nations Rugby Songbook* will let you join a chorus of thousands, singing their hearts out and willing their team on to victory.

Bring it on!

David Morris

Hen Wlad Fy Nhadau

Mae hen wlad fy nhadau yn annwyl i mi,
Gwlad beirdd a chantorion, enwogion o fri;
Ei gwrol ryfelwyr, gwladgarwyr tra mâd,
Tros ryddid gollasant eu gwaed.

Cytgan:
Gwlad, gwlad, pleidiol wyf i'm gwlad,
Tra môr yn fur i'r bur hoff bau,
O bydded i'r heniaith barhau.

Hen Gymru fynyddig, paradwys y bardd;
Pob dyffryn, pob clogwyn, i'm golwg sydd hardd
Trwy deimlad gwladgarol, mor swynol yw si
Ei nentydd, afonydd, i fi.

Os treisiodd y gelyn fy ngwlad dan ei droed,
Mae hen iaith y Cymry mor fyw ag erioed,
Ni luddiwyd yr awen gan erchyll law brad,
Na thelyn berseiniol fy ngwlad.

(Evan James 1809-78)

Literal translation:
The old land of my fathers is dear to me,
Land of poets and singers, famous men of renown;
Her brave warriors, very splendid patriots,
For freedom shed their blood.

Chorus:
Nation [or country], nation, I pledge to my nation.
While the sea is a wall to the pure, most loved land,
O may the old language endure.

Old mountainous Wales, paradise of the bard,
Every valley, every cliff, to me is beautiful.
Through patriotic feeling, so charming is the murmur
Of her brooks, rivers, to me.

If the enemy oppresses my land under his foot,
The old language of the Welsh is as alive as ever.
The muse is not hindered by the hideous hand of treason,
Nor is the melodious harp of my country.

Sosban Fach

Mae bys Meri-Ann wedi brifo,
A Dafydd y gwas ddim yn iach.
Mae'r baban yn y crud yn crio,
A'r gath wedi sgrapo Joni bach.
Sosban fach yn berwi ar y tân,
Sosban fawr yn berwi ar y llawr,
A'r gath wedi sgrapo Joni bach.

Dai bach y sowldiwr,
Dai bach y sowldiwr,
Dai bach y sowldiwr,
A chwt ei grys e mas.

Mae bys Meri-Ann wedi gwella,
A Dafydd y gwas yn ei fedd;
Mae'r baban yn y crud wedi tyfu,
A'r gath wedi huno mewn hedd.
Sosban fach yn berwi ar y tân
Sosban fawr yn berwi ar y llawr
A'r gath wedi huno mewn hedd.

Dai bach y sowldiwr,
Dai bach y sowldiwr,
Dai bach y sowldiwr,
A chwt ei grys e mas.

Literal translation:
Mary-Ann has hurt her finger,
And David the servant is not well.
The baby in the cradle is crying,
And the cat has scratched little Johnny.
A little saucepan is boiling on the fire,
A big saucepan is boiling on the floor,
And the cat has scratched little Johnny.

Little Dai the soldier,
Little Dai the soldier,
Little Dai the soldier,
And his shirt tail is hanging out.

Mary-Ann's finger has got better,
And David the servant is in his grave;
The baby in the cradle has grown up,
And the cat is 'asleep in peace'.
A little saucepan is boiling on the fire,
A big saucepan is boiling on the floor,
And the cat is 'asleep in peace'.

Little Dai the soldier,
Little Dai the soldier,
Little Dai the soldier,
And his shirt tail is hanging out.

Calon Lân

Nid wy'n gofyn bywyd moethus,
Aur y byd na'i berlau mân:
Gofyn rwyf am galon hapus,
Calon onest, calon lân.

Cytgan:
Calon lân yn llawn daioni,
Tecach yw na'r lili dlos:
Dim ond calon lân all ganu--
Canu'r dydd a chanu'r nos.

Pe dymunwn olud bydol,
Hedyn buan ganddo sydd;
Golud calon lân, rinweddol,
Yn dwyn bythol elw fydd.

Hwyr a bore fy nymuniad
Gwyd i'r nef ar adain cân
Ar i Dduw, er mwyn fy Ngheidwad,
Roddi i mi galon lân.

(Daniel James 1848-1920)

Literal translation:
I don't ask for a luxurious life,
The world's gold or its fine pearls,
I ask for a happy heart,
An honest heart, a pure heart.

Chorus:
A pure heart full of goodness
Is fairer than the pretty lily,
None but a pure heart can sing,
Sing in the day, sing in the night.

If I wished for worldly wealth,
It would swiftly go to seed;
The riches of a virtuous, pure heart
Will bear eternal profit.

Evening and morning, my wish
Rising to heaven on the wing of song
For God, for the sake of my Saviour,
To give me a pure heart.

Myfanwy

Paham mae dicter, O Myfanwy,
Yn llenwi'th lygaid duon di?
A'th ruddiau tirion, O Myfanwy,
Heb wrido wrth fy ngweled i?
Pa le mae'r wên oedd ar dy wefus
Fu'n cynnau 'nghariad ffyddlon ffol?
Pa le mae sain dy eiriau melys,
Fu'n denu 'nghalon ar dy ôl?

Pa beth a wneuthum, O Myfanwy,
I haeddu gwg dy ddwyrudd hardd?
Ai chwarae oeddit, O Myfanwy
Â thanau euraidd serch dy fardd?
Wyt eiddo im drwy gywir amod,
Ai gormod cadw'th air i mi?
Ni cheisiaf fyth mo'th law, Myfanwy,
Heb gael dy galon gyda hi.

Myfanwy, boed yr holl o'th fywyd
Dan heulwen disglair canol dydd.
A boed i rosyn gwridog ienctid
I ddawnsio ganmlwydd ar dy rudd.
Anghofia'r oll o'th addewidion
A wnest i rywun, 'ngeneth ddel,
A rho dy law, Myfanwy dirion,
I ddim ond dweud y gair 'Ffarwél'.

(Richard Davies 1833-77)

Translation:
Why is it anger, O Myfanwy,
That fills your eyes so dark and clear?
Your gentle cheeks, O sweet Myfanwy,
Why blush they not when I draw near?
Where is the smile that once most tender
Kindled my love so fond, so true?
Where is the sound of your sweet words
That drew my heart to follow you?

What have I done, O my Myfanwy,
To earn your frown? What is my blame?
Was it just play, my sweet Myfanwy,
To set your poet's love aflame?
You truly once to me were promised,
Is it too much to keep your part?
I wish no more your hand, Myfanwy,
If I no longer have your heart.

Myfanwy, may you spend your lifetime
Beneath the midday sunshine's glow,
And on your cheeks, O may the roses
Dance for a hundred years or so.
Forget now all the words of promise
You made to one who loved you well,
Give me your hand, my sweet Myfanwy,
But one last time, to say 'farewell'.

Cwm Rhondda

Wele'n sefyll rhwng y myrtwydd
Wrthrych teilwng o'm holl fryd:
Er mai o ran yr wy'n adnabod
Ei fod uwchlaw gwrthrychau'r byd:
  Henffych fore
Y caf ei weled fel y mae.

Rhosyn Saron yw ei enw,
Gwyn a gwridog, teg o bryd;
Ar ddeng mil y mae'n rhagori
O wrthrychau penna'r byd:
  Ffrind pechadur,
Dyma'r llywydd ar y môr.

Beth sydd imi mwy a wnelwyf
Ag eilunod gwael y llawr?
Tystio'r wyf nad yw eu cwmni
I'w gystadlu a'm Iesu mawr:
  O! am aros
Yn ei gariad ddyddiau f'oes.

(Ann Griffiths 1776-1805)

Translation:
Lo, between the myrtles standing,
One who merits well my love,
Though His worth I guess but dimly,
High all earthly things above;
Happy morning! Happy morning!
When at last I see Him clear!
When at last I see Him clear!

Rose of Sharon, so men name Him;
White and red his cheeks adorn;
Store untold of earthly treasure
Will His merit put to scorn
Friend of sinners! Friend of sinners!
He their pilot o'er the deep.
He their pilot o'er the deep.

What can weigh with me henceforward
All the idols of the earth?
One and all I here proclaim them,
Matched with Jesus, nothing worth;
O to rest me! O to rest me!
All my lifetime in His love!
All my lifetime in His love!

Bread of Heaven

Guide me, O Thou great Jehovah,
Pilgrim through this barren land.
I am weak, but Thou art mighty;
Hold me with Thy powerful hand.
Bread of heaven, bread of heaven,
Feed me till I want no more;
Feed me till I want no more.

Open now the crystal fountain,
Whence the healing stream doth flow;
Let the fire and cloudy pillar
Lead me all my journey through.
Strong Deliverer, strong Deliverer,
Be Thou still my strength and shield;
Be Thou still my strength and shield.

When I tread the verge of Jordan,
Bid my anxious fears subside;
Death of deaths and hell's destruction,
Land me safe on Canaan's side.
Songs of praises, songs of praises,
I will ever give to Thee;
I will ever give to Thee.

(William Williams 1717-91)

When the Coal Comes from the Rhondda

When the coal comes from the Rhondda,
And the water's running fine,
With my little pick and shovel,
I'll be there!
When the coal comes from the Rhondda,
And the water's running fine,
With my little pick and shovel,
I'll be there!

I'll be there! I'll be there!
With my little pick and shovel,
I'll be there!
When the coal comes from the Rhondda,
With my little pick and shovel,
I'll be there!

On the gallows number nine,
And the water's running fine,
With my little pick and shovel,
I'll be there,
On the gallows number nine,
And the water's running fine,
With my little pick and shovel,
I'll be there!

I'll be there! I'll be there!
With my little pick and shovel,
I'll be there!
When the coal comes from the Rhondda,
With my little pick and shovel,
I'll be there!

I Bob Un Sy'n Ffyddlon

I bob un sydd ffyddlon
Dan Ei faner Ef,
Mae gan Iesu goron
Fry yn nheyrnas nef.
Lluoedd Duw a Satan
Sydd yn cwrdd yn awr:
Mae gan blant eu cyfran
Yn y rhyfel mawr.

Cytgan:
I bob un sydd ffyddlon,
Dan Ei faner Ef,
Mae gan Iesu goron
Fry yn nheyrnas nef.

Meddwdod fel Goliath
Heria ddyn a Duw;
Myrdd a myrdd garchara
Gan mor feiddgar yw;
Brodyr a chwiorydd
Sy'n ei gastell prudd:
Rhaid yw chwalu'i geyrydd,
Rhaid cael pawb yn rhydd.

Awn i gwrdd y gelyn,
Bawb ag arfau glân;
Uffern sydd i'n herbyn
A'i phicellau tân.
Gwasgwn yn y rhengau,
Ac edrychwn fry;
Concrwr byd ac angau
Acw sydd o'n tu!

(Henry Lloyd (Ap Hefin) 1870-1946)

Literal translation:
For everyone who is faithful
Beneath his banner,
Jesus has a crown
Above in the kingdom of heaven.
Hosts of God and Satan
Are now clashing:
The children have their lot
In the great war.

Chorus:
For everyone who is faithful
Beneath his banner,
Jesus has a crown
Above in the kingdom of heaven.

Intoxication like Goliath
Challenges man and God;
Imprisons myriads and myriads
Being so audacious;
Brothers and Sisters
Are in its castle of sadness:
Its fortresses must crumble,
All must be set free.

Let us meet the enemy,
Everyone with holy weapons;
Hell is opposed to us
With its pikes of fire.
Let us press into the ranks,
And let us look up;
The Conqueror of the world and death
Is with us on every side!

Hymns and Arias

We paid our weekly shilling
For that January trip:
A long weekend in London,
Aye, without a bit of kip.
There's a seat reserved for beer
By the boys from Abercarn:
There's beer, pontoon, crisps and fags
And a croakin 'Calon Lân'.

And we were singing hymns and arias,
'Land of my Fathers', 'Ar hyd y nos'.

Into Paddington we did roll
With an empty crate of ale.
Will had lost at cards and now
His *Western Mail*'s for sale.
But Will is very happy
Though his money all has gone:
He swapped five photos of his wife
For one of Barry John.

And we were singing hymns and arias,
'Land of my Fathers', 'Ar hyd y nos'.

We got to Twickers early
And were jostled in the crowd;
Planted leeks and dragons,
Looked for toilets all around.
So many there we couldn't budge –
Twisted legs and pale:
I'm ashamed we used a bottle
That once held bitter ale.

And we were singing hymns and arias,
'Land of my Fathers', 'Ar hyd y nos'.

Wales defeated England
In a fast and open game.
We sang 'Cwm Rhondda' and 'Delilah',
Damn, they sounded both the same.
We sympathised with an Englishman
Whose team was doomed to fail
So we gave him that old bottle
That once held bitter ale!

He started singing hymns and arias,
'Land of my Fathers', 'Ar hyd y nos'.

So it's down to Soho for the night,
To the girls with the shiny beads;
To the funny men with lipstick on,
With evil minds and deeds.
One said to Will from a doorway dark,
Damn, she didn't have much on.
But Will knew what she wanted,
Aye… his photo of Barry John!

'Cos she was singing hymns and arias,
'Land of my Fathers', 'Ar hyd y nos'.

© Max Boyce

Delilah

I saw the light on the night that I passed by her window,
I saw the flickering shadows of love on her blind.
She was my woman,
As she deceived me I watched and went out of my mind.

My, my, my, Delilah,
Why, why, why, Delilah?
I could see that girl was no good for me,
But I was lost like a slave that no man could free.

At break of day when that man drove away, I was waiting,
I crossed the street to her house and she opened the door.
She stood there laughing,
I felt the knife in my hand and she laughed no more.

My, my, my Delilah,
Why, why, why Delilah?
So before they come to break down the door,
Forgive me Delilah, I just couldn't take any more.

She stood there laughing,
I felt the knife in my hand and she laughed no more.
My, my, my, Delilah,
Why, why, why, Delilah?
So before they come to break down the door,
Forgive me Delilah, I just couldn't take any more;
Forgive me Delilah, I just couldn't take any more.

(Reed/Mason)

We'll Keep a Welcome in the Hillside

Far away a voice is calling,
Bells from memory do chime;
'Come home again, come home again,'
They call through the oceans of time.

We'll keep a welcome in the hillside,
We'll keep a welcome in the Vales.
This land you knew will still be singing
When you come home again to Wales.

This land of song will keep a welcome
And with a love that never fails,
We'll kiss away each hour of *hiraeth*
When you come home again to Wales.

(Lyn Joshua and James Harper. First published 1943)

SWING LOW ....

God Save the Queen

God save our gracious Queen,
Long live our noble Queen,
God save the Queen!
Send her victorious,
Happy and glorious,
Long to rain over us;
God save the Queen!

Jerusalem

And did those feet in ancient time
Walk upon England's mountains green?
And was the holy Lamb of God
On England's pleasant pastures seen?
And did the Countenance Divine
Shine forth upon our clouded hills?
And was Jerusalem builded here
Among these dark Satanic mills?

Bring me my bow of burning gold!
Bring me my arrows of desire!
Bring me my spear! O clouds, unfold!
Bring me my chariot of fire!
I will not cease from mental fight,
Nor shall my sword sleep in my hand,
Till we have built Jerusalem
In England's green and pleasant land.

(William Blake 1757-1827)

Swing Low, Sweet Chariot

Chorus:
Swing low, sweet chariot,
Coming for to carry me home;
Swing low, sweet chariot,
Coming for to carry me home.

I looked over Jordan and what did I see?
Coming for to carry me home,
A band of angels coming after me,
Coming for to carry me home.

Sometimes I'm up and sometimes down,
Coming for to carry me home,
But still my soul feels heavenly bound,
Coming for to carry me home.

The brightest day that I can say,
Coming for to carry me home,
When Jesus washed my sins away,
Coming for to carry me home.

If I get there before you do,
Coming for to carry me home,
I'll cut a hole and pull you through,
Coming for to carry me home.

If you get there before I do,
Coming for to carry me home,
Tell all my friends I'm coming too,
Coming for to carry me home.

Abide With Me

Abide with me; fast falls the eventide;
The darkness deepens; Lord with me abide.
When other helpers fail and comforts flee,
Help of the helpless, O abide with me.

Swift to its close ebbs out life's little day;
Earth's joys grow dim; its glories pass away;
Change and decay in all around I see;
O Thou who changest not, abide with me.

Not a brief glance I beg, a passing word;
But as Thou dwell'st with Thy disciples, Lord,
Familiar, condescending, patient, free,
Come not to sojourn, but abide with me.

Come not in terrors, as the King of kings,
But kind and good, with healing in Thy wings,
Tears for all woes, a heart for every plea,
Come, Friend of sinners, and thus bide with me.

Thou on my head in early youth didst smile;
And, though rebellious and perverse meanwhile,
Thou hast not left me, oft as I left Thee,
On to the close, O Lord, abide with me.

I need Thy presence every passing hour.
What but Thy grace can foil the tempter's power?
Who, like Thyself, my guide and stay can be?
Through cloud and sunshine, Lord, abide with me.

I fear no foe, with Thee at hand to bless;
Ills have no weight, and tears no bitterness.
Where is death's sting? Where, grave, thy victory?
I triumph still, if Thou abide with me.

Hold Thou Thy cross before my closing eyes;
Shine through the gloom and point me to the skies.
Heaven's morning breaks, and earth's vain shadows flee;
In life, in death, O Lord, abide with me.

(Henry Francis Lyte 1793-1847)

Amazing Grace

Amazing grace, how sweet the sound,
That saved a wretch like me.
I once was lost but now am found,
Was blind, but now I see.

'Twas grace that taught my heart to fear.
And grace, my fears relieved.
How precious did that grace appear
The hour I first believed.

Through many dangers, toils and snares
I have already come;
'Tis grace that brought me safe thus far
And grace will lead me home.

The Lord has promised good to me.
His word my hope secures.
He will my shield and portion be,
As long as life endures.

Yea, when this flesh and heart shall fail,
And mortal life shall cease,
I shall possess within the veil,
A life of joy and peace.

When we've been here ten thousand years
Bright shining as the sun,
We've no less days to sing God's praise
Than when we'd first begun.

(John Newton 1725-1807)

LOW LIE THE FIELDS OF ATHENRY

Amhrán na bhFiann
(A Soldier's Song)

Sinne Fianna Fáil,
atá faoi gheall ag Éirinn,
Buíon dár slua
thar toinn do ráinig chughainn,
Faoi mhóid bheith saor
Seantír ár sinsear feasta,
Ní fhágfar faoin tíorán ná faoin tráill.
Anocht a théam sa bhearna baoil,
Le gean ar Ghaeil, chun báis nó saoil,
Le gunna scréach faoi lámhach na bpiléar,
Seo libh canaig amhrán na bhFiann

Soldiers are we
Whose lives are pledged to Ireland;
Some have come
From a land beyond the wave.
Sworn to be free,
No more our ancient sire land
Shall shelter the despot or the slave.
Tonight we man the gap of danger
In Erin's cause, come woe or weal
'Mid cannons' roar and rifles' peal,
We'll chant a soldier's song.

(Peadar Kearney 1883-1942, Irish lyrics by Liam Ó Rinn)

Ireland's Call

Come the day and come the hour,
Come the power and the glory,
We have come to answer
Our country's call
From the four proud provinces of Ireland.

Chorus:
Ireland, Ireland,
Together standing tall;
Shoulder to shoulder,
We'll answer Ireland's call.

From the mighty Glens of Antrim,
From the rugged hills of Galway,
From the walls of Limerick
And Dublin Bay,
From the four proud provinces of Ireland.

Hearts of steel
And heads unbowing,
Vowing never to be broken,
We will fight, until
We can fight no more,
From the four proud provinces of Ireland.

(Phil Coulter)

Molly Malone

In Dublin's fair city
Where the girls are so pretty,
I first set my eyes on sweet Molly Malone
As she wheeled her wheel-barrow
Through streets broad and narrow,
Crying 'Cockles and mussels, alive, alive, oh!'

Chorus:
'Alive, alive, oh,
Alive, alive, oh',
Crying 'Cockles and mussels, alive, alive, oh!'

She was a fishmonger
And sure 'twas no wonder,
For so were her father and mother before,
And they each wheeled their barrow,
Through streets broad and narrow,
Crying 'Cockles and mussels, alive, alive, oh!'

She died of a fever
And no one could save her,
And that was the end of sweet Molly Malone.
Now her ghost wheels her barrow
Through streets broad and narrow,
Crying, 'Cockles and mussels, alive, alive, oh!'

CONTENTS